InBetween Shadows

InBetween Shadows

by

A<small>NN</small> B<small>AILEY</small>

Order this book online at www.trafford.com
or email orders@trafford.com

Most Trafford titles are also available at major online book retailers.

© Copyright 2011 Ann Bailey.

All rights reserved. No part of this publication may be reproduced, stored in a retrieval system, or transmitted, in any form or by any means, electronic, mechanical, photocopying, recording, or otherwise, without the written prior permission of the author.

Printed in the United States of America.

ISBN: 978-1-5521-2618-9 (sc)
ISBN: 978-1-4122-4274-5 (e)

Trafford rev. 04/25/2011

 www.trafford.com

North America & International
toll-free: 1 888 232 4444 (USA & Canada)
phone: 250 383 6864 ♦ fax: 812 355 4082

DEDICATED TO

THOSE WHO DIED SO THAT

OTHERS MAY LIVE

To

my husband

and

Rick Wheeler

who both died in 1992

JUNE 13 1944

She showed their tickets at the Gate to a grey haired man dressed in a grubby looking railway uniform. He clipped them and handed them back to her.

'Train leaves in seven minutes, Madam', he informed the woman who was nervously searching for the porter who had taken her luggage

He appeared behind her, luggage piled onto a trolley. 'I'll put 'em in the luggage compartment, you just go and find yourselves a seat', he suggested, staring at the ground as she fumbled in her purse for two thrupenny bits.

The child looked angrily at her mother, she liked thrupenny bits, twelve sided brassy coins which she collected in a specially shaped money box. She thought a sixpence would have served the purpose.

'You will be careful to put them on the right train', she asked, anxiously.

'Don't you worry, Madam', he mumbled, disappointed at his tip.

She felt uncomfortable at the thought of their luggage disappearing without her superintending its safe storage. After all, she told herself, losing clothes was like losing the family silver, what with rationing. She dismissed her thoughts for there were seats to be found on a train full of soldiers. She took her child's hand and hurried along towards the engine at the far end of the platform where pistons were hissing and an occasional puff of grimy smoke rose from the funnel.

'Here's a place, quick get in before it's taken', the child felt a hard hand on her back as her mother tried to hurry her into the carriage.

'May I sit here', she inquired, politely. 'She can sit on my lap, she's so small and far too thin', she added, confirming this triviality more to herself than to the soldiers who were trying to manoeuvre themselves into the narrow seats.

'You can have my seat, ma'am', offered a handsome young soldier. ' I don't mind standing in the corridor, I can talk with my friends and get a cup of tea'.

'If you're sure'.

'My pleasure ma'am'. He slid the carriage door open and disappeared down the corridor.

She settled back and gave a sigh of relief as the Guard at the back of the train gave a final blast on his whistle and late passengers slammed carriage doors. The train jolted as its wheels slid on the track before slowly moving forward.

She stared out of the window at the passing countryside. She had not noticed the war in Wales, everything had seemed reasonably normal except for her sister who believed in herbal tea and ghosts. She looked down at her child and smiled with satisfaction.

They had enjoyed their holiday together, her sister's cottage was old with a thatched roof and lots of nooks and crannies and creaking floor boards. There was an orchard and her daughter had climbed trees and they had paddled and netted small fish in a stream running at the bottom of the garden. Lambs and sheep had bleated all night in a nearby field and her sister, in her usual outspoken manner, had told her child that was because they sensed they were to be slaughtered.

Her daughter had run to her room and thrown herself on the bed. 'I'll never eat lamb again', she swore, too young to understand the impossibility of her oath. 'I hate farmers, how can they do that', she had sobbed.

And what was even worse, her sister had gone on about the cottage being haunted and she had been angry with her and told her not to speak like that in front of a child. But her daughter had seemed to take it in her stride and told them how she often saw ghosts.

'Rubbish', she had snapped fiercely, indicating the subject was closed.

She turned her attention to a young soldier sitting opposite, he seemed little more than a school boy and she wondered if he missed his mother and how his mother must have felt losing her son to a war, so far away. She watched him as he took a chocolate bar and began to break it into small pieces but he stopped when he became aware of her daughter staring at it with large eyes and a half open mouth. He felt in his pocket.

'Would you like a bar?', he offered.

She felt obliged to refuse but he insisted and she gave in easily.

'Don't eat it all at once', she warned her child who had no intention of taking her mother's advice.

She returned to the young soldier. 'Where do you come from', she asked, curiously.

'California, ma'am'.

'Los Angeles?', she asked, hopefully.

'No ma'am. A little more to the east.

'I've always wanted to live in America but my husband will never move, war or no war', she sighed again, as though accepting her dreams would never be fulfilled. 'My husband is building airfields for you Americans over in Norfolk. He comes home every three weeks with a big tin of ice cream. They wrap it in lots of newspapers to keep it cold', she rambled on.

'That must be nice for your family'.

'I go to the cinema every week', she boasted. 'I just love Fred Astair and Ginger Rogers'.

The young soldier laughed. 'Yea, my mom also likes them'.

The child was aware of her mother's animated conversation and wondered if she really did want to go to America and whether her father also went to romantic films while he was in Norfolk.

'You can imitate Carmen Miranda, can't you', she turned her head towards her child. 'Show the kind soldier what you can do'.

Her daughter sat frozen at her mother's request. 'Go on then, you do it so well'.

The child held out for as long as she could but she knew it was hopeless. She stood between the squashed legs of the young soldier and her mother and with wriggling hips and her arms swirling above her head, she tried to sing with a Brazilian accent.

'I,yi,yi,yi,yi, I love you very much,
'I,yi,yi,yi,yi, I think you're grand'.

She fell back in her seat when she was finished, obviously wishing she could disappear for she held her comic in front of her face for the rest of the journey.

After what seemed an eternity, the green fields and hedgerows turned to broken fences, untidy gardens used as allotments and bomb damaged houses and workshops. The frivolous conversations had slowly fallen away and the soldiers in the corner seats slept with their heads resting on the dirty windows, their legs sprawled out between each others.

'We're almost there', she informed the soldiers as she sighted the fleeting name of a railway station.

She was reaching for her basket on the rack above her when the sound of an enormous explosion threw her off-balance so that she fell across the young soldier sitting opposite. She pulled herself off him, steadied herself, and resumed her composure by brushing down her navy blue suit and straightening her white summer hat.

'That must be the gas works going up', she gasped, hazarding a guess.

The young soldier stood up, 'I guess it's going to be a long war, ma'am', he said softly.

The child noticed his clouded eyes and a piercing pain travelled from her heart to her throat for she could feel his fear.

Her mother touched the soldier's hand, 'God Bless you', she whispered.

She turned away feeling overwhelmed by impending tragedy.

JULY 29 1944

    The young soldier threw himself face down onto the ground as the inevitable carnage and debris from explosions rained down on him. He could hear someone swearing profusely at the dark forms of aircraft flying high overhead. A soldier stood up and shouted profanities while he shook a clenched fist violently at the sky.
    'Get down you bloody idiot', yelled one of his friends, but his words were lost in the blast of red fire which consumed him and his comrades lying on the muddy ground. The now fatally wounded young man gasped for breath and asked himself why was he in this hell, where was God and, above all, where was his mother.
    The next blast was different, it was white, silver white. A white which seemed to wash over him, soothing the pain from the last blast and followed by a silence he had never known before, though he thought he could faintly hear a child singing, 'Jesus bids us shine with a pure clear light, like a little candle burning in the night'.
    He stood up painfully and brushed himself down. A stifling misty dust hung all around and he waved his hand in front of his face in the hope of clearing the air but it was too thick as though sticky from explosives and smouldering fire. He called out in the hope of hearing a voice, even a scream or a moan, but there was nothing, not even his dragging steps made a sound as he crawled over the rubble of shattered trees and hedgerows. Nothing seemed to break the eerie stillness which now engulfed him with fear.
    He could not tell how long he staggered through the debris but suddenly his hopes were raised as he caught a glimmer of light, a dim beam, maybe from a jeep or armoured vehicle which became brighter as he determinedly moved towards it. He

would be saved, he need not fear anymore and a feeling of peace enshrouded him as he sunk back onto the muddy ground and gave himself up to whoever it was waiting for him.

He was lying on his back when he woke up, the mist had cleared and above him was an endless deep blue sky, endless to eternity, he thought.

It was some time before he saw his mother standing in front of their house while his brothers played baseball on the roughed up grass. He sighed with relief, he was safe. He had made it home.

APRIL 27 1991

He pulled his dressing gown from off the chair and crept downstairs as silently as he could. She was still asleep and he relished the early morning quiet, his first cigarette and the smell of freshly ground coffee dripping through the filter while he read the daily newspaper. When he was ready, he would take her a cup before she began her day which consisted of a great deal of activity and chatting over irrelevancies. He did not mind, she was lively. 'Never a dull moment', he murmured, as he shook the newspaper out and glanced at the headlines. Later, he thought it was not a particularly special morning, in fact it promised not to be.

She was standing on the landing almost breathless when he arrived with the coffee. 'You'll never believe this', she gasped, before he could put the cup down.

'Believe what?'

It seemed to him that she had experienced some kind of dream about American soldiers. It was hard to follow but he listened attentively to her unbelievable story and could only suggest she should write it down. What else could he say, it would serve no purpose to tell her to be realistic and logical, she was far too worked-up for that.

And then there was this middle-of-the-night writing business which she called the 'Writings'. He thought another man might have been irritated but his philosophy regarding marriage was based on an easy life, for he had long learnt that making small ripples could often result in large waves.

He thought, at least for the time being, he would stand on the side line without committing himself one way or another. In fact, he was not at all sure whether her so-called 'Writings' were exactly what she said they were.

After all, there could be a God, who was he to say!

She had insisted they should go to Normandy to find the graves or, at least, to visit St. Lô where her forefathers had originated. He had agreed. After all, it was not too big a sacrifice sitting on a sunny terrace with a bottle of good wine watching the world go by, watching the girls go by. The change might even make him feel a bit better.

EVENTS FROM APRIL 1991 TO THE PRESENT

It was my family who suggested I should write down everything that happened in 1991 and 1992. Eventually, in 2001, I published a book called 'InBetween Shadows'. Now, in 2011, ten years later, I am trying again to reach those who would like to have reasonable proof of a life after death.

It was on Saturday morning, April 27, 1991, when my suspicions of the existence of a spirit world were confirmed. The story I am about to tell you is factual and documented. 'June 13 1944' is my memory, a detailed memory, and although 'July 29 1944' holds a degree of 'Writer's License' it is, in essence, correct.

I hope my story and 'Writings' might convince you that there is another dimension, another life, a place of love and peace.

There was nothing unusual about that morning, I was lying in bed, half awake, remembering a visit to Victoria, Canada, many years before. We had visited the "Sealand" and watched the Orca whales jumping through the water. As I remembered their glistening black bodies I felt just as though I was there, present in the past, and could even feel the water splashing my face. It was at that moment, I saw in my vision two American soldiers standing to the left of me. Although I was terribly shocked l was able to realise that I must keep them with me by not opening my eyes or moving. I knew they were without high rank and killed outside St. Lô, Normandy, France, during the Second World War. I asked them their names.

The soldier nearest to me told me his name very clearly. The other soldier gave me two names either one of them could have been a Christian or a Surname, such as Peter James or Paul Thomas but one of the names was similar to his friend's name for example John and Johnnie. The second soldier told me that his 'friend' died in the first week of his war and that he died later. I saw them so clearly I am still able to remember how they looked.

Perhaps, I should now mention that I had been searching my family tree and had recently found that my forefathers had left St. Lô around 1690. They were French Huguenots (Protestants) who fled to London fearing persecution in Catholic France.

It was also during this time that I began, during the night, to write religious prose some of which I made into poems. I do not know whether there is a connection between the appearance of these two unknown soldiers and these 'Writings' but it seems coincidental that they occurred at the same time.

I was totally excited when eventually my husband came upstairs, after the soldiers' appearance, and his reactions were in hindsight amazing. He not only listened but encouraged me to begin a search, this time not for my past family but for two U.S. soldiers killed in 1944.

I contacted the U.S. Embassy who informed me that the Normandy Cemetery was at Coleville sur Mer, just behind the Omaha invasion beach.

My husband and I arrived there on May 24 1991 and immediately went to the Visitors' Building which contained books listing all military personnel buried overseas. It must be very different now with online information. It was easy to find the soldier who had clearly given me his name. He was a Private First Class killed on July 4 1944, in Normandy.

The other soldier was slightly more difficult to find owing to the interchangeable names. However, he was a Private First Class, killed on July 29 1944, in Normandy. Both soldiers had graves numbered twenty-one.

The soldiers belonged to the 83rd Division, VII Corps, 330 and 331 Infantries and landed on Utah Beach on June 26. The soldier who was killed on July 4 did die in the first week of his war.

July 4 and July 29 are the birthdays of my two daughters. Just a coincidence! But it was because of this coincidence

I decided to search further. It took me one year to find two brothers of the soldier killed on July 29. I was unable to find personal details of the other soldier since many records were destroyed by fire in the National Personnel Records Centre in St. Louis, Missouri, in 1973. However, this soldier joined the army in Tyler, Texas, in November 1940. And, of course, I have his Service number.

During my year's search I contacted several U.S. army and civil organisations.

Mortuary Affairs and Casualty Support Division
National Personnel Records Centre
Vital Statistics Section
Historical Services Division
An Attorney at Law's office
A public library in Texas
A local newspaper

I wish to thank all the people in these military and private organisations who were so kind and helpful.

During my search, I obtained maps showing the positions of these Infantries on July 4 and 29. Both were to the west of St. Lô.

Eventually, I received a letter from the two brothers, written on April 12 and posted on April 13 1992, stating that my 'happening' appears to be accurate. I telephoned them around August the same year and they told me that their younger brother had, indeed, been killed outside St. Lô by his own bombers. A tragic mistake.

On April 8, 1992, my brother living in Victoria, Canada, telephoned to tell me that his son-in-law, Rick Wheeler, a soldier in the Canadian army, had been killed in a tragic accident while on a training exercise near Medicine Hat, Alberta. He died on April 7 and was buried on April 13. The day the letter from the brothers was posted to me. Both Rick and the U.S. soldier were killed by their own people.

I was overcome by the feeling that there was a connection, no matter how small, between these deaths so I contacted my brother to ask Christina, Rick's wife, for information regarding his Service number etc.

I set below a list of coincidences :

The U.S. soldiers were killed on the birthdays of my two daughters (July 4 and 29)

Both U.S. soldiers had Grave number 21.

The U.S. soldier killed on July 29 had 8 numbers in his Service number. Rick Wheeler had 9.

When you add up the 8 numbers you get a total of 48. When you add up the 9 numbers you also get a total of 48.

The U.S. soldier was killed in 1944. Rick Wheeler was killed in 1992, 48 years between their deaths.

The U.S. soldier was 19 when he died, Rick Wheeler was 29. Together they add up to 48.

Both soldiers were killed tragically by their own military.

Family of the U.S. soldier posted a letter to me on the day of Rick's funeral, April 13.

The 330 Infantry sailed on the 'Orion' and the 331 Infantry on the 'George Washington'. Both boats sailed from New York Harbour on April 6 1944, arriving in England on the April 19. Perhaps one or both of them sailed after midnight on April 6, the day Rick died!

When I tell people this story, their first reaction is 'why Americans?' I have never been able to answer this question. The only time I met American soldiers was on a train to London and that journey stood out for three reasons.

Firstly, my mother made me do a song and dance act, imitating Carmen Miranda, in front of a carriage full of American soldiers which was mortifying for an eight year old. Secondly, because the first V I rocket was dropped on June 13 just as we were about to arrive in London. I can remember the sound of the explosion. Because of this I am able to pinpoint the day we left Wales. Thirdly, our luggage got lost which caused my mother to panic. Luckily, it was found later.

According to the Internet, the U.S. soldiers were stationed at either Adderley Hall, near Market Drayton, Shropshire or at Tarporley, Cheshire. They trained in North Wales and The Midlands for about two months before leaving for the south of England.

Is it possible I shared a carriage with American soldiers from the 83rd Division, on June 13, 1944? This is the only unproven detail in my true story.

On May 30 1994, I met up with the 83rd Division, 330 and 331 Inf. at the Henri Chapelle American Cemetery in Liege, Belgium, in the hope I might find someone who knew one of my soldiers. Unfortunately, it was not to be but they did confirm how their Infantries had been surrounded just outside St. Lô. They had sent up smoke signals which were carried away by the wind. Their aircraft missed their target and they were bombed by mistake.

I live in the Netherlands so the journey to Liege was reasonable.

After Rick Wheeler died, my niece in Canada asked me to try to 'contact' him and I did for one year. He seemed to take me through his life. He showed me his little pony, brown with a white blaze down his nose; how he and his school friends, one called Jeff, had a near drowning accident; that his school teacher had a Scandinavian name, it was Mr. Olson; how he won a little brown jug at a fairground during a soccer match; how he shot targets at fairgrounds with the gun against his left shoulder to make it more difficult; how he had trained at White (Horse) Pass on the border of Alaska and British Columbia and how he had once been bitten by a mosquito on the left side of his nose which became infected.

Christina had to ask Rick's family in Nova Scotia and his army friends if these incidences were correct, they were. It was she who persuaded me to self-publish my story and 'Writings' and worked hard in 2001 to get my book printed. Not to forget my husband who supported me, faithfully, during my search in 1991 and part of 1992.

To sum up, I believe there are three questions to be asked. Firstly, did it happen? Secondly, if it did, then why? Thirdly, what had the death of two U.S. soldiers in 1944 have to do with the death of Rick Wheeler in 1992?

To answer the first question, it either did or did not happen, there is no half way. If it did not happen then it was a dream followed by multiple coincidences. If it did happen, and I know it did, then so many coincidences could prove the existence of another dimension!

The second question, Why? Maybe, to comfort Christina and me on the forthcoming deaths of our husbands. Perhaps I crossed paths with the U.S. soldiers on the train. Perhaps it was to make me pay attention to the 'Writings' which I received in 1991.

The third question is perhaps the most important. If it were not for the tragic death of Rick then my account of the 'Appearance' of the American soldiers would be without substance.

It could be said I had made it up! Certainly, with the information now available on Internet this would be possible but there was no Internet as such in 1991 and I have, of course, correspondence dating back to that time.

I try not to theorise over why Rick Wheeler died when he did and all the coincidences surrounding his death. Speculation is just what it is, 'speculation'. But whatever conclusions readers might draw, I know I saw the two U.S. soldiers on April 27 1991. I know there is another dimension of life when we die simply because I have had contact with many spirits.

Those who contact me do not give advice or send messages but rather transfer thoughts of photographs or scenes of past events so that they can be recognised, sometimes they even give their names. And it seems their purpose is to give comfort to those they left behind.

I have, over the years, tried to convince people who doubt that there is a Godly power, a Universal Knowledge, whichever word you wish to call this Divinity. If the 'Writings' came from the spirits in the Universe then they must have a Universal Truth, timeless, touching the very essence of our Being.

Of course, I question and rationalise, especially when I see photographs of the unending expanse of the universe in all its diversities. However, my search for Truth has only led me to Belief and to the certainty that there is only one Supreme Spirit, one God, and we can follow different prophets and call Faith by different names but in the end we are worshipping the same Deity.

My hope is that someone, somewhere, is helped by the 'Writings' which is, I believe, the purpose they were given to me. If I can help just one person then I have fulfilled my task.

TODAY

She sat back and stared at her laptop. She knew the story she had just written inside out and back to front, she had lived with it for twenty years, not that she had thought of it every day but just once in a while when she was 'contacting' other spirits. She did not consider herself to be a Medium, not someone sitting across a table hoping to help some heartbroken client searching for comfort.

She did not consciously work at receiving her Spirits, they came when they wanted without encouragement from her. She found that if she noticed someone for no particular reason then she would, most likely, have contact with their loved one. This would be followed by the urge to ask the person in question whether they knew someone who etc. etc. She was usually right and it gave her a 'buzz', a good feeling.

The U.S. soldiers' appearance had shocked her for they had 'jumped' in, even startling her. She did not know them or anyone connected to them and finding them became an obsession. She had, in hindsight, written excited letters to military organisations and waited with baited breath for their answers. Sometimes, it had taken longer than she had hoped but she had got there in the end.

Now, after all these years, there were two new points she would like to prove. The first, whether either the 'George Washington' or the 'Orion' left New York Harbour on April 7 1944 and not April 6, perhaps one or both of them were delayed by logistic problems, the tide, or whatever else delays 'Time of Departure'. She felt that somewhere in a dark musty corner of a basement there might be a file showing the exact time the boats sailed. If only one of them left N.Y. on April 7, then it would be yet another coincidence to add to the list of all the others. Seeing how Rick had died on that date.

She thought her second point would be impossible to prove but if proven would give her the right to shout from the hill tops. She was aware that time was running out but there could still be someone who might remember travelling on a train from the North of England, probably from Crewe, to London on June 13 1944. Perhaps, a World War II veteran, from the 83rd Div. VII Corps. remembers watching an eight year old do a Carmen Miranda song and dance act. For, as vague as it might sound, unimportant incidences stay in the memory of people who are stressed and those soldiers were only a few weeks from landing on the Normandy beaches and full-out war.

Or, perhaps a soldier wrote something in a letter home about his journey to the south of England to replace the miserable news he had to tell his loved ones.

She sighed, all wishful thinking she thought. But there again, a Divinity had been involved twenty years ago and she knew anything was possible, if so wished by some greater power.

She closed her laptop,

'WRITINGS'

and

POEMS

FEBRUARY 24 1991

I scatter His Words as he who sows
his seeds upon the fertile land.
And I wait for His Words to take root and
yield its harvest in abundance.

For I say, each minute seed is as great as
the plant which bore it.
No seed is too small or a breeze too light to carry it.
For His Words are both great and small and
each Word bears fruit, just as the smallest seed.

And when the crop is ripe the reaper will cut it
and store it, so he may feed upon its goodness,
and the seed of the harvest will multiply again,
forever in eternity.

FEBRUARY 24 1991

And He has great lands, so great that when
you climb the mountains you cannot see its limits.

And some of His lands are less fertile than others,
so He sends His helpers to those lands and they tend
them and see that they are watered and nourished
and become as fertile as their neighbours.

And even land that is poor because it is stony has a purpose
for it too yields what it can.
For His helpers take every stone away and bring them to
a place where they may be sorted and placed in
His house.

And His helpers travel all their lives and no land is too far
for them to go.

So, I say, even the stones on His lands have a place in
His Kingdom.

FEBRUARY 24 1991

And do not the great trees shed their leaves and
branches and do you not use the leaves to enrich
your earth and the branches to warm your house.
Therefore, is not each small leaf and branch used?
So is it in His Kingdom.
Each is as great as the great tree itself for surely
it too was once small. Is not then great and small equal?
For in my Father's Kingdom there is no difference
between the two.
For each creature is necessary to the other and each was
made with a great purpose, for there is a plan in all that
was created.
Therefore, let no man break the intended plan for it was
the original and only the Creator may judge the purpose
of all things.
Remember that even the sun does not rise or set if the
Creator does not wish it, neither the rise and fall
of the great tides for even they must wait for the moon.
All creation then is in balance with itself and only Man
destroys his own existence and, surely, this must be
judged by the Creator.

Keep then what is perfect, perfect. For Man and all other
was born so.

FEBRUARY 26 1991

And I say to you, write His words so they may
be read and spread around the world.
For the world is filled with sounds that drown
His words.
Silence these sounds and listen, for to hear is to Know
and to Know is to Be and to Be is to live in Peace.

Let silence then be louder than all other and
let that silence be heard for His voice is silent
and must be listened to with great care.

Let then those who roar be still so those who
dare not speak, may speak.
For surely, those without a voice must have much to say.

Let then those who tread heavily walk softly,
so those without steps may walk and their tread be heard.
For surely, they have a place to go.

Therefore, in His name, I say to those
without a voice or a tread have Faith in what He says.
For surely, the voice of our Father
must be heard and then you will also be heard,
if only for one minute, or one second,
which in the House of Our Father is for Eternity.

MARCH 1991

And He spoke and His words were carried
over the mountains, down the valleys,
across the plains and seas.
Whispers in the wind, never lost,
listen and you will hear.

For His words having been spoken are never lost.
His footsteps having crossed the desert dust, still must
for they can never not be.
Only covered by the sands of time
waiting for the soft wind of Truth to blow them bare.
Printed for Eternity.

And He spoke and His words were heard by some,
and those who would not hear were as the deaf
and shook their heads and went their ways.
But the wind still carries His words,
never silent, only unheard.

MARCH 1991

The door to my room has closed and
I may not re-enter, but it is of no matter
for another door has opened and before
me are endless horizons.

And where I travel is where I must be,
I take no step that has no purpose
or destiny.

I do not seek neither do I desire and all
wanting and despair have ceased and all
that the flesh demanded is quiet.

For in my room I was my own prisoner,
I was my own keeper and guarded my
own freedom as a captive is guarded.

Now I walk the pastures and stand upon
mountains I could never climb.
Here I can neither tire nor fall,
nor hunger nor thirst, for I am fulfilled.

APRIL 1991

His coat will never be divided
neither by war nor storm,
for it comforts and warms those
who will shield under its greatness.
And he who stands under it
shall not fear, nor bend his head,
nor be meek, nor reviled by others.
For the strength of its cloth
shall protect and unite those by His side as one.
And the one shall be great and stand firm
against the enemy till he turns and retreats
back into his darkness.

Message

His Word has been spoken by your words,
your interpretation limited by your good Faith,
an erring rationalism which restricts
the boundaries of human thought.

APRIL 9 1991

And He passed me by on the road
to Galilee and seeing that I stared,
beckoned me and said,
'Follow me'.

And I walked within His footsteps,
rested within His shadow and
supped at His table.
And He broke bread and said,
'Eat to fill your body,
listen to fill your soul'.

And I ate and I listened and though
my body still hungered my soul
was filled for time everlasting.

APRIL 9 1991

I hunger, yet I have eaten,
I thirst, yet I have drunk.
Fill me so I may fill others
and sit with them around the table of Faith
where hunger and thirst are unknown.

Messages :

God is the all-embracing Sight
and the Creation, which is His Perception,
is in its centre.
A visual testament confirming
the Creator's eye.

APRIL 9 1991

And the crowds were restless for there was
no food and His followers said,

'Feed them Master, for they hunger'.

And He turned to the crowds and said,

"I cannot fill your bodies but I can fill your souls.
For is it not better to fill the needs of the soul
than that of the body?
What does it matter if the body hungers
for it is not with you in the next world.
But a hungry soul will hunger forever in Eternity".

And my hunger left me for it was only of the body.

Message

God is Sublime Perfection
and you have restricted yourselves
by naming Faith.
But no denomination has this right,
for the Spirit has no name or appendage.

APRIL 20 1991

Do not fear when the time comes
for it is but a single step,
so small and yet a stride.
Do not fear the enclosing dark
for dark is but the reverse of light.
Do not fear pain for you will know not of it.
Do not fear loss for those you have lost
will be again.
Do not fear emptiness for here you will be filled.
For where you are now is but a slow death,
here is a living new life where you will not seek
fulfilment for it will be yours.
Nor will you seek love for as you love
so will you receive.
An eternal chain of eternal love in eternal light.
For here there is no difference in any Man
whether it be his station, his colour or his creed.

So rejoice, for whether you be the greatest
or the smallest the door is open to all
and the entrance is the same for all.

For I tell you so as Keeper of all things,
both Here and There.

APRIL 22 1991

And I dared not raise my voice for fear
of persecution, so I stood in the shadows
and listened to His words.

But when I heard His Belief and saw
His bravery I was filled with strength,
uncaring of my own life but marvelling
only in His Glory.

So I spoke up, no longer fearing ridicule
and death but filled only with the desire
to tell the world what I knew.

Go, then, fear not the words of the Unbelievers
and tell those who are both blind and deaf,
to see and hear.

For the salvation of one is the salvation
of many, and nothing is impossible for
those with His Knowledge.

APRIL 22 1991

Be as the Reaper and work the land
and bring home the harvest.
Be as He who sows and waits for
the new shoots and prays for sun and rain.

But know that a good harvest will cost
you much toil and pain which will be
repaid at the final hour of reaping.

For when the sun finally sets after
the last straw has been cut and stood to dry,
Glory will fill you and the pain
of the cutting and binding will be gone
and fulfilment will be forever.

Message

It is not the time you take
nor the distance you go,
for the one complements the other.
Therefore, small steps will complete
the course as well as large.

MAY 4 1991

You ask, so I will tell.
You will say you understand
but you will not.
For your question is that of all Men
from their beginning to their end.
For you will be the Fire and the Water,
the Faith, the Hope, the Charity
and yet more.
You will be at one with creation,
both Parent and Child.
You will be All within All,
at one with All.
And in your oneness you will be
everything, everywhere,
unseen, unheard.
Being in your Unbeing.

And you have asked and I have told,
and you have understood without understanding.
For the dimension is not within your power
to understand, nor will you understand when
you are within that dimension;
only accepting what is,
forever in Eternity.

AUGUST 5 1991

Seek until you find the Absolute and never
quench the thirst for Knowledge nor suffice
the hunger for Understanding.

For if these are satisfied then you will no
longer seek and can never be sure that
you have found the Truth.

And teach those who do not seek and
travel with those with Faith until you find
the Knowledge which lies at the end
of the road to the greatest Kingdom of all,
where you may rest forever.

AUGUST 1991

And when I came before the Light I wept
for I had never seen such beauty.
And I knew that all before had been as an empty
cup waiting to be filled.

And I was ensouled with its perfection and a love
I had never known and an understanding of all
things I had never understood.
And I wept for those who knew not of it.

And I stepped forward to enter its greatness
but could make no movement for it was not I
who may choose my destiny within.
And I waited without and even that was more
than I had ever known before.

And patience and stillness entered my soul
and the waiting was a fulfilment which I had
unto never known.

And I wept with happiness that I may wait
even if it were to be for Eternity.

AUGUST 10 1991

Cast not your net too far for the catch need not
be more than can be handled by any one man.
For those who are nearby can hear
the best and those too far away must
strain to hear, and if the Word is
too light upon the air will lose interest
and turn away, being lost forever.

Is it not better then to tell those who hear well
so they may further the Words,
so keeping the strength of the Source.

Be then His fisherman and catch those waiting
to be caught and bring to them the Faith,
which is the Hope they have lost or never had.

Be then His Source and see that the rivers
and streams carry your Words and cover
the lands, a flood of Truth which enriches
the soil and bears strong crops.

For the one is the other, as the fish that swim
in the waters which come from the Source,
which is He.

SEPTEMBER 3 1991

And I saw them resting beneath the shading trees
for the sun was at its highest and they talked and
laughed over all things; fish and cattle, heat and rain,
arid and fertile land.

And I saw Him raise His hand to stop their
further discourse and He said.

'Be as the Shepherd and lead your flock to those
green pastures even though the path is difficult
and wearisome. And count each sheep for to lose
one is to show defeat to the prowlers who wait
for the weak and struggling.

So guard them rather than those who walk
with the flock and when the pastures are reached
you may rest and watch with love those who feed.

And expect no payment for the Shepherd
has no needs other than to bring his flock to safety.

DECEMBER 8 1991

For to seek is to find,
to travel is to arrive,
to love is to lose.
For as we give another takes
and when we have no more to give
we will arrive from whence we came.
Then in our oneness we will be as many
for the many are themselves as one.

DECEMBER 27 1991

And I climbed the mountains and crossed
the plains and before me were the clear waters
of the timeless river and, because I thirsted,
I cupped my hands and drank of it.

And He who was on the other side of the river
called and beckoned me to cross the waters
and though I feared the deep, I walked with trust
into the clear shallows.

And He, who had beckoned, beckoned once
more and I waded on though fearful of the deep
before me. And when at last I floundered,
I called to Him on the other side for help but
He only beckoned and gave no hand.

And so I struggled on until I reached the other
side and only then did He, who had called,
hold out His hand.
And I asked Him why had He not helped me in
my desperate struggle for life and He answered,

'I beckoned and I called and you came,
but the way you take is yours,
be it not enough that I wait'.

OCTOBER 21 1998

Death is but a continuation of life
which is the materialisation of the mind
and body after its conception by the spirit.

Therefore, a spirit may enter an earthly
form to accommodate its necessities
for a specific period of time and which
returns to its Source when no longer needed.

JANUARY 18 2001

And even if God is only the personification of nature,
would you then not cling by your fingertips to the roots
of simple grass in the hope of Salvation.
Whichever way you look at it, you will always cry out
to God when in need, when fear clutches your hearts.
And if you do not cry for God then which man will not
cry for his mother, but she too is in the womb of God.
There is no escaping God for He is the Creation and the
Re-creation. God is the womb of Creation.

SOFTLY, SOFTLY

SOFTLY, SOFTLY

Softly, softly, I call to you,
listen to what you cannot hear,
see what is not within your sight,
use time as though the end were near.

Then tell the world what they cannot hear,
show them what they cannot see,
for in their blindness is My light,
in their deafness is My voice,
in their denial is My eternity.

LIFE BOAT

I am drifting on uncertain seas,
pounded by every merciless wave,
trying to hold the rudder of Truth
so I may by Belief be saved.

Let doubt not alter my chartered course
but let Hope billow into my sails,
let Faith be my guiding star,
let me find Peace in the ocean's swell.

THE DREAM

Last night I dreamed I walked a path,
singular and straight,
and at the end I saw a Light,
shining white, as only God can make.

And in my dream He was the Light,
excellent and just,
and when I heard Him call my name
I lowered my head for I felt my shame.

For I dreamed He loved me with all my faults,
my mind with all its impure thoughts.
I dreamed He loved me for who I am
and for what I am not.
He loved me as we humble beings cannot.

So as I stood with arms outstretched
empty of all worldly goods,
I dreamed He loved me without terms
as only He the Almighty could.

JUST AS I WAS

Why do they see me so pale and serene,
my skin as smooth as butter cream,
my hair hanging down as a golden sheath,
why am I so seen for our Belief?

While my husband carved at his wood all day,
I cleaned and cared while he was away.
And I picked and spun the wool from the sheep
and worked in the fields to help earn our keep.
And I stood at the loom, our cloth to weave,
and toiled, as all women, from morning to eve.
And my love was not only for my first born, my son,
but for all of my children, I loved them, each one.

So why do they paint me so blond and so pale,
why do they worship a woman that's white and so frail?
Far better to love me just as I was,
a daughter of Israel
who bore also her Cross.

GOD IS LIFE

God is life, all life,
from the murmuring of the wind
to the rustling of the trees,
from the roaring of great oceans
to the trickling of small streams.

God is life, mine and yours,
filled with sweet delights
to the meanest daily chores.

He gives and takes,
I must hurry before life comes and goes
and then it will be too late !

THE MOTHER

She held her new child to her breast
His hair still wet with blood,
she held His clenched hand to her lips
and kissed the child of earth.

She knew this child, born of love,
was for the world to die,
so they may see and feel the light,
she kissed Him as He lie.
And with every precious passing year
she watched her child grow strong,
she watched Him love His fellow men
and lead them away from wrong.
And when it was His time to leave,
she stroked her son's dark hair,
she held His strong hand to her lips
and kissed with loving care.
And every year they were apart
her heart was torn asunder,
three years waiting anxiously,
each year brought some new wonder.
And when at last they had their way
and He was taken from the Cross,
she held her brave son in her arms
and dearly wept our loss.

She held her child to her breast,
His hair still wet with blood,
she held His limp hand to her lips
and kissed the Man, our Saviour.

LET ME DO BATTLE

If I have a task then let me fulfill it,
let me beat the drum and follow
the insignia of Your Peace.
Let me not fear the darkest chasm
or the highest peaks for there are
those along the way whose hearts
will be touched, even if secretly.
And if it is Your intent so it will be
for Your Will will be my strength
to lead the smallest army to conquer
the greatest foe.

END OF THE TUNNEL

I travelled long to find this place,
stumbled over uneven ground,
tripped and fell along the way
but now I stand triumphant,
my new life begins today.

For I have reached the light,
magnificent and chaste,
it fills me with a love unknown,
lightens the corners of my mind
and soothes my earthly pains.
And I rejoice,
for in my death, I live again.

PURE SPIRIT

Oh, pure spirit, flame of light,
moving gently through my mind,
give me wisdom of ages past,
let truth be always within my grasp.

Lead me to good away from wrong,
lead me to light away from dark,
be my comforter and my guide,
greet me when I reach the other side.

CHILD OF BETHLEHEM

I walked across the sands of the Holy Lands,
I preached outside unfriendly city walls,
I defended My Belief before the learn'ed men
for I was the boy child born in Bethlehem.

I fished upon the timeless seas of Galilee
and shared the catch with those who were without,
I supped with men who listened to My words
and with My blessings spread the Hope they heard.

I hung upon a crude cross at Calvary
so you may make the world a better place,
but still I hear you utter fierce cries of war
and still the Dove of Peace cannot soar.

I shed My blood so you may heal your wounds
and forgive those who wish to do you ill.
I gave you Faith so you may not fear the night,
I gave My life so you may live in Light.

I SOAR BETWEEN

I soar between
where cool sky meets warm earth,
where rising mist carpets lush green fields
and chasing winds sweep across the ground,
swirling dry leaves,
round and round.

I wing between,
where expectant crops await the promised rains,
where glaring sun tears open dusty soil
and children wait to die on fruitless land,
their half-closed eyes
full of flies and sand.

And where I am, I weep,
for I cannot make the cloudless skies form rain,
nor stop the floods that soak the ripened grain,
nor can I help those without a choice,
nor can I, the Dove of Peace,
find rest until the world is one.
Only then can I Rejoice.

WITH THE WIND

'Come with me', said the wind,
'and I will take you to the light'.
And he gently wrapped me in
in his warm breath
and I lay there sleeping
in my new life, my death.

And he took me to where I had to be
a place beyond, neither land nor sea.
A place where mortals cannot tread,
a place of life for those now dead.
A place without sickness, sorrow, sadness,
a place of compassion, mercy, gladness.
A place without famine, strife and war,
a place where anger is no more.
A place of friendship, no one a stranger,
a place of safety, no earthly danger.
A place so wondrous it pains the heart,
a place forever, no end, no start.
A place of love for eternity,
a place of life for perpetuity.

FILL ME WITH WORDS

Fill me with words, so I may spread Your word,
give me Knowledge, so I may give others Knowledge.
Let me understand Your creation
so I may be at Peace with it.
Let me understand time so I may use it correctly,
let me understand the nature of all things
so I may be at one with nature itself.

I am, but you do not see,
I call, but you do not listen.
Why then do you say you are forsaken
for I am the day and the night.
the light in the dark
and the shadow that falls.
How then can I not Be if all other is.

CHRISTIAN DEEDS

If I could but print a step so true and firm
that another man may say,
"here stood he from whom we learned,
here was his shadow cast,
here spoke he words of Love and Hope
that in our hearts do last".

Then when I come before you, Lord,
my mortal case to plead,
I may say I served you, Sir,
with worth by Christian deeds.

A UNIVERSAL PRAYER

Oh, Lord, give us the courage to accept that
which cannot be changed.
Give us the strength to change that
which can be changed.
Give us the wisdom to know the one
from the other.

THAT'S LIFE

InBETWEEN SHADOWS

The watery day is slowly closing
and the sun forms thin shadows across the lawn,
uncut, soggy, autumn forlorn.
And mist creeps over the leafy earth
and clings to spidery webs, fine spun,
silhouetting each perfect cord,
daylight is ending, my day's just begun.

For now I will close my windows and doors
and set the ready-laid fire ablaze
and sit and read and laze and gaze
at the flickering flames and feel smug,
without any shame.

Oh, sweet autumn, Inbetween days,
not yet icy, not warm from sun's blaze,
but Inbetween weather with Inbetween light
and it seems the world is a little more quiet,
and mellow and calm, twix living and dead,
full of Inbetween shadows cast by
Inbetween sun, Inbetween red.

POPPY LOVE

Come with me and we will climb that hill
where we can see the coloured fields below;
patchwork quilt.
And when we reach the top
out of breath, sticky hot,
I will spread a rug upon the swaying grass
and we will lie as lovers do,
and wish the sky would cover us
with sheets of heavenly blue.

And when shadows fall too long and thin
and farewell feelings stir within,
I will pick a wild flower,
just one simple bloom,
red as my blood that runs for you.
Dark is my flower's centre
as my thoughts when we must part,
Oh, Poppy of the summer fields
let my love, love me
and let my black thoughts pass.

WEDDING DAY

Today we have vowed never to part
today we have touched each others' heart.
Today we have worn our wedding rings
and promised to love whatever life brings.
To stand by each other through fire and water
and when times are bad to try not to falter.
To be thankful when our lives seem right
and to keep our goals in clear sight.
Not to hurt when we can be kind
to each others' needs, not to be blind.
To try to give and not to take
and to build and not to break.
To always be true
and not to delude.
To say I'm to blame
and say it without shame.
To listen to the other side
and not behind our ego's hide.
To try to accept each others' faults
and not to think with bad thoughts.
And when we go to bed each night
to try to think of all that's right.
Today we have given each other our hearts
today we have vowed never to part.

TO LOVE

I will make a bed of love
smooth white sheets
pristine clean
pillows of soft down between.
Crowns of Purity.

Love blinding
bodies merging
minds entwining
passion flowing.
Lost Virginity.

Lives shared
sorrows bared
feelings bruised
words soothed.
Happy in Unity.

THE GUARDIAN

Each baby I've held to my breast
has always been the very best
that God could give me as a gift.
And as I kissed that little face
I prayed that He would grant me Grace
to be its faithful guardian.

REGRETS!

I rejected the one who cared,
I chased the devil who dared.
Now I must pay the cost
of the angel that I lost.
And all I can do is dream
of how life might have been!

I'LL BE THERE WAITING

I awaken startled, something's amiss,
I try to recall my senseless dreams
but I'm as blank as a page, unwritten, clean.
There is something I must know or do,
there is something that is false or true,
then suddenly I remember, I think of you.

Half-lying, I watch the unsettled dust,
particles dancing in translucent beams,
swaying and swerving in light bands seen.
And I gently ponder over you,
as a speck of dust one day you'll fall
and I'll be there waiting, no rush at all.

IF I MUST LOSE YOUR LOVE

If I must lose your love, then let it be now.
Let us part before our love is scathed
by great lies and careless deeds,
scheming plots to deceive,
for we still live as dreamers' dream.

If I must love your love, then let it be now.
Let us part before doubt creeps
between the covers of our content,
cooling warm love spent,
for I will not see your morning scorn.

If I must lose your love, then let it be now.
Let us part before delusion dawns
before we slash the silken night
with wounding words till brittle light,
for I will not hear you patronize.

If I must lose your love, then let it be now.
Let us part before we fight and hate
fraying hearts so tightly ravelled,
breaking threads we can't untangle,
not love's design, not yours not mine.

TIME'S CLOCK

Each night I sleep for just a while,
not too long, and waken gently
as though I have been pulled
from where I was.
And in those moments of return
fear clutches my heart,
for time cannot read a clock,
nor count the swinging arm.

Tick, Tock, I know one day
I'll have a shock.

FAMILY FIGHT

She stands alone at the kitchen sink
with tears in her eyes that quite make her blink.
They roll softly down her pale tired face
and she wears her clothes with so little grace.

He is late, as always, never at home,
working or drinking or cleaning car's chrome.
She hears the car's engine, he's come home at last
and she feels her neck tensing, she ready to blast.

'I'm home, dear', he calls, friendly and normal,
she answers in tones that are clipped and formal.
And he knows, so well, her cool off-hand act,
so he keeps a low profile and awaits her attack.

He can see her gun's loaded, war is declared,
so he sits down quite calmly, fully aware
that this will enrage his poor pent-up mate
and he schemes very carefully without any hate.

'Have a nice day, dear', he asks with a smile,
such a kindly remark will be good for a snarl.
She has bitten the bait and comes back for more,
he's used to her nagging and quite knows the score.

She's fires the first bullet from her pointed gun
and he grins to himself for he hasn't begun.
For his tactic is silent and cool and too smug
and he knows this campaign is what her will bug.

Rat-a-tat-tat, rat-a-tat-tat,
round after round, he knows it off pat.
Now she is crying, she's used her last bomb,
so heightens himself with manly aplomb.

He rat-a-tats back for just a short while
but does it controlled in a neat, off-hand, style.
The war's nearly over, peace will come soon,
perhaps after dinner and an evening of gloom.

Tomorrow, he'll bring a present or two
and offer to take her and the kids to the zoo.
And now she will sit and watch the tv
and he'll do the washing up and make her some tea.

SINGLE TRACK

We bought two one-way tickets
and boarded the train of love,
we left the gritty city
for green hills and blue above.
But later there was a tunnel
and the driver forgot the lights
and when it was all over
I was alone in the clear daylight.
Now I wait by the ticket office
to board the train of love
and if I should be so lucky
I'll see green hills and blue above.
Then the lover who sits beside me
must try to understand
that when we reach the tunnel
I'll grab him by the hand.
Yes, I'll hold onto my lover
so he cannot change his track,
so he cannot board another train
when sweet light turns black.

LOST LOVE

Our love did run its fickle course
and no matter how we tried
we could not live our lives a lie.
Now when we meet our fingers touch,
just briefly, never able to firmly clutch.
Then we smile and kiss, as friends do kiss,
waiting for some spark of bliss,
waiting for love's flame to light,
but nothing happens and we stay polite
and walk on, ever knowing of the other.

OCEAN LOVE

Our love is as the sea
sweeping endlessly to and fro,
moving constantly as our passion
from our highs to our lows.
Sometimes pounding upon the shores
angry and full of spite,
then later rippling on a beach
as if repentant, quite contrite.

Our love is as the tide
turning with every mood,
holding secrets in its depths
allowing no one to intrude.
Every current pulling us
from deep love to shallow hate,
never knowing where we are
as floating flotsam on a sea of fate.

Our love is as the moon
changing endlessly its shape,
hanging prisoner in the ether
unable to escape.

For passion is as timeless
as the moon in orbit caught,
back to when the earth was silent
when God and Satan fought.

TRUE PERCEPTION!!

When you say you love me truly
my heart is filled with fear,
for your Truth is your Perception
and Perception is not always True!

TO THE BETTER HALF

Why is love Pie in the Sky
why can't love always bring us that high!
Why can't I be honest and not so deceptive
why must you change what you've already accepted!
Why can't I be calm, settled and sure
why must you want that little bit more?
Why must I learn to think as you do
why must you smile when I feel too blue?
Why must I be your perfect reflection
why should you demand my undying affection!
Why can't I consider your finer feelings
why must you suffer my 'wheelings and dealings'!
Why can't we nurture love's magic spell
why must you make my life living hell?
Why can't we tell of our love every day
is there anything else more important to say?

THE TURBULENT GAME

We are trapped in a web we ourselves spin
of achievement, success and wanting to win.
We are under a mountain of human rubble,
mortgages, leases and even each other.
Trapped by the goodies that modern life brings,
bright lights, fast cars and beautiful things.
And when it's all over, we are as we came,
naked, alone, as each other, the same.
And I wonder if we could do it again
would we still want to play in that turbulent game,
or would we just sit back and let life slide by
and watch all the others and smile as they sigh!

TO MY CHILDREN

Each night as I laid in my soft warm bed
and the house was quiet at long last,
I thanked you God for the day that had been
and another safe day that had passed.

I watched them each day come tumbling from school,
dishevelled and noisy, without any cares,
I watched them each day as they gobbled their tea
and bickered and whined, 'it's not fair'.
And come rain, wind or shine they went out to play
in the mud by the edge of the lake,
where they entered a world they created themselves
and their clothes were a constant headache.

I watched them each day as they grew to full youth,
their bodies so straight and so strong.
I watched them each day as they hurried their meals
and rushed to the clubs they belonged.
I was told all good parties began after ten
to café's and disco's they went,
where they entered a world they created themselves
sleepless nights were for me too frequent.

I watched them each day commuting to work,
a sobering up I perceived,
I watched them each day as they paved the same way
as their forefathers, daddy and me.
Like a flock of young birds they sought out their mates
and made love in the dark of the night,
where they entered a world they created themselves
and returned home to prepare for their flight.

Each night as I lay in my soft warm bed
and the house is quiet at long last,
I thank you God for the years that have been
and I pray for the years not yet passed.

PARADISE LOST

I have to hang my head in shame
when I see how Man's to blame
for what he's done to his home
the earth,
the most beautiful planet
in the Universe.

I pray to all that is good and pure
whatever profit, whatever lure,
to stop this madness before it's too late
if only for our children's sake.

A SUGGESTION BY A GRANDSON

His young grey eyes looked up brightly
as only new eyes can.
'I would take a match box', he suggested,
'and put his photo in it.
That way you can put him under your
pillow every night and sleep with him'.

I gazed silently at my small friend,
his simplicity making me realise that
I could no longer think clearly.
How my mind had become a tangle
of complicated flashing pictures,
nothing fitting, no puzzle completed,
just darting, jangling memories and lurking fears.

Maybe in time, I will again see it simply,
the time when they will sit me in a chair
and try to forget I am there.
Then I will think and remember as a child
and will be, once again,
rich in my innocence.

LET'S PUT IT BACK

Oh, what a pity the world didn't stand still
for it's too full of people and too full of ills.
For there's too many planes in the skies overhead,
too many species of animals dead.
Too many cars, too much traffic,
too many walls painted with graphic.
Too many bottles and too many cans,
too much litter spread over the land.
Too many chemicals dumped in the oceans
too many people supporting this motion.
Too many nitrates seep through the land
too much sewerage washed up on the sand.
Too many trees chopped for mankind
too few 'Green Laws' agreed and signed.
But when we get down to the bottom line
it's not you or me who commit the real crime.
For the multinationals have too much at stake,
these and our governments do our earth really rape.
For where there's big money and economies involved
will problems like these ever get solved?
So let's put it back, just as before,
we don't ask for much and we won't ask for more!

JUDGEMENT DAY!

I do not fear, should I?
Must I fear my life because I fear my death,
when dark will one day fall
upon my struggling breast.

And if there is a nothing,
then nothing have I to fear,
but if there is another life,
then this life might cost me dear!

Perhaps I'll have a Counsel to plead
my careless deeds,
perhaps I'll have an Orator to defend
my greedy needs.

Perhaps they'll be a Jury
to weigh life's tinsel and brash glitter
and hope, for me, the scale not tilt
too low with feelings hurt and bitter.

Well, perhaps, I fear a little bit
for hard as I may try
I cannot live my life so well,
but that's twix God and I.

FAMILY DIVORCE

After such a long time
I saw my grandchild for one hour,
perhaps a little more.
My heart sung as it broke,
simultaneous loss and gain,
an unbalanced ledger, my pain.

And I am stilled by it
a thing so large hanging over
a child so small.

And only time can change the sum
when merging feelings come to one.
And they will.

PAST LIVES

We seek past lives, lives we have lived before,
perhaps not once but many times more.
We strain to remember past lived places,
objects, deeds, familiar faces.
To remember that which we cannot quite,
to remember that now out of sight.

Yet sometimes we have a fleeting knowing,
a split-second glimpse, a flashing showing.
But when we look it is not there,
like a handful of mist it's gone, gone where?
Back from whence it came,
back to the recesses of our forgetting brains!

RIVER OF LIFE

We are as streams
created pure from source,
sucklings born of Mother Earth
trickling down the easiest course.
But as we broaden each flowing mile
dark clouds loom over distant hills
and obstacles deflect our path,
barriers to our free-loving Will.

And slowly we are no longer clear
as we rush between the laboured lands,
no longer sure of our destiny,
no longer sure of our Maker's plan.
So while we flow to maturity
we carefully measure each alien turn,
conscious of every meandering mile
sensible to what we must learn.

Then when we feel the time is right
to take the chance to fulfil our needs,
gathering strength we roar along,
determined only to succeed.
Deep canyons conquered, great falls leaped,
we stride the land as some mythical God,
ruling the valleys and mountain sides,
ambitions filled, innocence lost.

And when we've run our impeded course
and completed all that laid ahead,
low-lying lands and placid plains
will gently ease the force we had.
There we can judge what we lost and gained,
what we did learn since our simple start
when we were full of youthful hope,
now softly flowing with Peace at heart.

WINTER THOUGHTS

Winter has come and I cannot love its beauty
for all is stilled, cold enshrined,
a time of death rather than of life
and I am robbed of Summer, warm and fine.

For now the fields are harsh and lonely,
and leaf striped trees stand stark and bare,
bending their heads with every fierce blast
under dark skies no shadow can cast.

But the bright winter robin, breasts red and aglow,
turns every promising blade,
throwing damp leaves to and fro
not caring the world is one dark shade.

But rather accepting the clouded days
and every watery shaft of sun
as one cold miserable day that is won.
If only I were as contented as he!

DUTCH LANDSCAPE

The biting cold wind whips my face
as I stand gazing out from the guarding dike
at ribbons of ditches slicing flat fields,
murky homes to slippery eels and pike.

And to where land and sky meet as one thin line
stretching as far as the eye can see,
landscape spread under hanging Dutch skies,
endless till broken by wind breaking trees.

And behind me grey water laps six-sided stones
salt sea turned 'brack' in the manmade lake
imprisoned by wondrous manmade locks,
nature now tamed for mankind's sake.

A land where beauty and plainness meet,
reclaimed, pumped dry, won from the sea,
desolate apart from bird and beast,
land mastered by Man, but forever, maybe!

NIGHT

Bright day has once more yielded to dark night
and with its defeat I surrender too,
laying I gaze at familiar forms
lit by a moon hanging too new.
So, I passively wait for the faint cold rays
to turn devious dark to friendly dim
when finally my blurred thoughts race
to places no one may intrude within.

And I happily succumb to a world of dreams
sinking me into unknown deeps
where I playback films, wild or calm,
fragmented acts in history seeped.
And there in veiled shadows
I capriciously dwell
till electronic beeps pierce
my flickering scenes,
forcing me back to reality,
forsaking my perchance dreams.

So, I meet the day and whatever it brings
impatient to wing into sweet night,
into the mystery that captures my heart,
free from rational logic daylight.

BAG OF DREAMS

Under my pillow I hide my dreams
in a bag of colour that fills my mind,
places and faces I do not know,
whispering shadows from long ago.

And as I sleep upon my dreams
mysterious figures drift in and out,
till morning breaks and the spell is broken,
obscure intrigues carefully unwoven.

Tonight, I'll clutch my bag of dreams
and sail away on sparkling waves,
lit by clouds of galaxy light
into unseen realms with magic in sight.

LAST ROLL CALL

Oh, yes, I know this place well
for I've been here before
stepping over debris
from another blood-spilt war.
For me it's too familiar,
for me the path's too known,
for me it makes no difference
which flag hangs limp, shell-blown.
There are no men commanding,
they lie in blood, dark red,
there is no little drummer boy,
he's lying long since dead.
Oh, yes, I know this battle ground,
oh, yes, I know my way,
that's why I step so easily
between each makeshift grave.
For century, after century,
I call each side in line,
then the bugler sounds reveille
and the drummer boy beats time.
And both sides stand together,
man to man abreast,

the Corporals and the Captains,
the Sergeants and the rest.
Then I march them out of battle
away from blood and pain,
away from shattering fire,
away from greed and gain.
I march them down the valley
in straight and orderly line,
I march them into Glory
Forever out in time.

Ann Bailey

YOUNG SOLDIER (First World War)

Oh, young soldier you did die,
not yet man, just not child.
You marched bravely into battle
banners hoisted, flags flying high,
waving in the wind so boldly,
heralding for you to die.

They told you dying for your Sovereign,
and Motherland you held so dear,
would bring peace to your loved ones
and military honours to your peers.
But as you laid in your dug out trench
with your gun so tightly clenched, the enemy
not yet man, just not child,
was lying dead next to you,
lying in water, mud, blood drenched.

The night before your last great battle
you both dreamed of love and home,
each unknowing of the fearful foe,
each wanting peace, some mercy shown.
And had you once met at some Pub or Bar,
drunk a beer and played some Pool,
would you, could you, have fired your gun,
would you have shouted out,
 'We've won'!

Did your death, the hero's test,
change the course of that dark day,
would the world have suddenly stopped
if you had both just walked away.

For now we are all friends again
and trade and visit each others' lands,
lazing on the enemy beaches,
flirting, holding sweet girls' hands,
living as you wanted to.

Oh, young soldier, you did die,
not yet man, just not child,
what would you say if you saw us now?

THE LOSS

When they told me you were dead
there was nothing but my bitter sorrow,
each day as empty as the last
and all there was, were lonely tomorrows.
And my heart broke on that dark day,
the day you left, the day you died,
alone, without me by your side
in another place, under another sky.
For I could not say goodbye to you
nor could I hold you in my arms,
nor run my hands through your hair,
nor let my salty streaming tears
fall with my kisses over your dear face.
You laid with others watching by,
unloved and cold,
and all I had was our last embrace.

Now I hold you in my dreams,
I see you in every silent shadow,
You are in my memories' fantasies
And I will love you always, forever.

LET ME FIND WORDS

Let me find words to speak of pure pleasure
whilst I gaze upon nature's trove of fine treasure.
Let me find words for trees hanging green,
summer's cool wrap, lush and serene.
Let me find words for flowers so wild,
Buttercups and Daisies, chains for a child.
Let me find words to enthuse over friends
whose beauty and colour to my garden do lend,
Pinks and Carnations and Lupines and Phlox,
Asters and Poppies and tall Hollyhocks.
And Roses and Snowdrops and Wisteria too,
Begonias and Freesias and Cornflower Blues.
Let me find words for summer's last sun
warming damp leaves before winter's begun.
Shining last rays on carpets of brown,
gold and soft orange, autumn's warm gown.

And if I could write with fine sounding words
over my garden, trees, flowers and birds,
I still could not tell of my full heart's content
or how nature perfected God's good intent.

RAINBOW FREE

The sun's bright rays touch crystal spray
and rainbows form within my mind
awakening my colourless thoughts,
tints created by Divine design.
And my free-loving spirit soars on high
drifting across the sparkling seas,
brilliant jewels set in silvery waves,
fires in oceans of ecstasy.

And I am filled with rainbow glory,
coloured arch I bow as thee,
my longing spirit now at peace
for I am as thee, Rainbow Free.

MY FRIEND

Who is he who hides between the twilight and the dawn
but never stops to see the day's new morn.
Who is he who casts a shadow on my dreams
and creeps into the darkness of my mind, unseen.
Who is he who wakens me at the magic hour of three
with the tapping at my window from the branches of the tree.
Who is he who stands with no word said
and has travelled through the light, so long dead.
Who is he who comes from times long past
and in this world his misty form can no shadow cast.
Who is he who makes me turn my head
for I can feel his presence and his silent tread.
Who is he who must to this earth return
for what reason my mind is unable to discern.

I know not who he is, this spirit from long ago
but I think he is my friend rather than my foe.
And when my time to part does come,
will he be my Guide,
will he gently take my hand
and lead me to the other side?
Where all things I will understand.

A SMALL BUNDLE FOR MY HUSBAND

JUST ONE MORE TIME

If you could hold me in your arms
just one more time
and I could hold your hand in mine
just one more time.
If I could run my fingers through your hair,
silver grey in soft fair,
just one more time.
If I could touch your lips and whisper words,
so often said, so often heard,
just one more time.
If you could feel my tears upon your cheeks
then you would know how deep I weep.
If you could make my dark night shine,
just one more time,
then I could live forever in sweet dream
and wait until we meet again
in God's time.

LOVE TORN

You gave me life, you gave me love,
I floated on cloud eight above.
I saw the sun shine brilliant gold
and it seemed that bells from heaven tolled.
I winged with birds through cool blue skies,
sweetly singing my love cries.
I soared so high I lost my breath
but my descent was my slow death.

Because of you I was reborn
but now you've left I am love torn.
Now every day it seems to rain
will I ever feel the same?

THE SEA GULL
(A bronze sculpture by my husband's grave)

You spread your wings
and arch your back and lift.
You make a small turn
and catching an upstream breeze
softly glide,
soaring, circling, sailing,
High and away.

And I wait
as a black dot,
a full stop.
Muted.

BLOOD RED SKIES

If I could sail a boat for you
I'd travel every sea.
I'd curse the storm and fear high waves
and pray to see a beach.
And in the calm I'd greet the sun
each time it rose anew,
a golden plate to place my heart
to let my blood run free.

Then I would paint each setting day
in red and rose for you.

ANOTHER YEAR

Another year, another day
and there is no joy,
no hip, hip, hurray!

For even now as I think of you
my walls come tumbling down,
leaving me in devastation,
groping hopelessly around.

For gone is the sun that warmed my heart,
the hanging moon that lit my dark,
the star which kept me on my path,
now all around is stark, no spark.

Another year, another day
there are no cheers,
no hip, hip, hurray's

TOUCHING THOUGHTS

Do you not see me in the mist
and my footsteps in the snow?
Do you not feel me in your tears
and my touch within your smile,
Do you not hear the words I whisper
before you wake?

Just touching fingertips,
a breath away.

WILL YOU COME AGAIN

And under shading trees I lie and stare
at the flickering sun between the green,
until in trance-like state I see again what was,
the then so-living you.
You alive and strong and kind,
not as me, half-dead from loss and pain
and wishing, wishing, I could do it all
once more again.

And will you come again, as now,
will you come again?
For you know I cannot bear the space you left,
I reach it with my fingertips and feel
the nothing which enfolds.
No earthly love to hold.
And if I could I'd pull you back to me,
tied down, not free,
just you with me.
If I could,
I would.